D0948835

FROM:

FRIENDS LOVE YOU,

WARTS AND ALL

Written and compiled by
Ruth Cullen

PETER PAUPER PRESS, INC.
WHITE PLAINS, NEW YORK

To my kick ace friends of today,
and my renegade friends for always—R.C.

See page 81 for photo credits

Designed by Karine Syvertsen

Copyright © 2006
Peter Pauper Press, Inc.
202 Mamaroneck Avenue
White Plains, NY 10601
All rights reserved
ISBN 978-1-59359-922-5
Printed in China
20 19 18 17 16

Visit us at www.peterpauper.com

FRIENDS LOVE YOU,

WARTS AND ALL

INTRODUCTION

Who needs fair-weather friends? It's when the chimps are down and the chickens come home to roost that we need our faithful friends the most. We don't have to earn affection by being purrfect; friends love us even when we have spinach stuck in our teeth.

This tribute to true friends features our role models for unconditional love—animals—demonstrating with humor and honesty what we value most in our friendships.

Whether life's path is bumpy or smooth sailing, our close friends don't horse around or play  cat-and-mouse games. They hound us with hugs while embracing our uniqueness whole hog. Because the truth is, friends really do love us, warts and all.

REAL FRIENDS WILL TELL YOU WHEN YOU HAVE SPINACH STUCK IN YOUR TEETH.

AUTHOR UNKNOWN

YOU AND I . . .

WE'RE ONE OF A KIND.

A FRIEND CAN
TELL YOU
THINGS . . .

YOU DON'T WANT TO TELL YOURSELF.

FRANCES WARD WELLER

THE SHORTEST
DISTANCE
BETWEEN TWO
FRIENDS IS A
SMILE.

IF FRIENDS
WERE FLOWERS,
I'D PICK YOU.

AUTHOR UNKNOWN

THE ARMS OF FRIENDSHIP

ENCIRCLE THE WORLD.

FRIENDS DON'T
JUST SHAKE
YOUR HAND,
THEY
HOLD IT.

Friends always seem to know their place...

RIGHT BY YOUR SIDE

THE BEST THINGS IN
LIFE AREN'T THINGS . . .

THEY'RE FRIENDS.

YOU GAVE ME
THE COURAGE TO
STAND ON MY
OWN FOUR FEET.

A friend is someone who helps you when you're down,

and if they can't, they lie
down beside you and listen

LIFE'S SWEETER WHEN YOU SHARE IT.

FRIENDSHIP IS BORN
AT THAT MOMENT WHEN
ONE PERSON SAYS
TO ANOTHER,

"WHAT! YOU TOO?
I THOUGHT I WAS
THE ONLY ONE."
C.S. LEWIS

A FRIEND IS A PRESENT YOU GIVE YOURSELF.

Robert Louis Stevenson

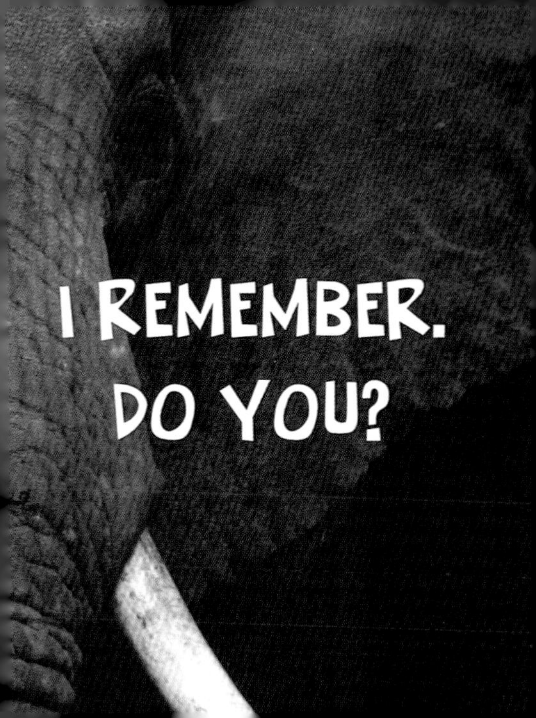
I REMEMBER.
DO YOU?

WHAT IN THE WORLD WERE WE THINKING???

FRIENDS ARE ANGELS
WHO LIFT US TO
OUR FEET WHEN
OUR WINGS
HAVE TROUBLE
REMEMBERING
HOW TO FLY.

AUTHOR UNKNOWN

MY FRIENDSHIP
WITH YOU YIELDS
RICHES BEYOND
COMPARE.

THE BEST FRIEND
YOU'LL EVER HAVE
IS **NOT** ALWAYS
THE ONE YOU AGREE
WITH THE MOST.

How will you know your REAL friends?

They're the ones
standing in
your corner when
everyone else
has left
the room.

YOU CAN WIN MORE FRIENDS WITH YOUR **EARS** THAN YOUR MOUTH.

AUTHOR UNKNOWN

FRIENDS HAVE
A WAY OF
PUTTING YOU
ON A PEDESTAL.

BEST FRIENDS
AREN'T AFRAID
TO GET PUSHY,

ESPECIALLY WHEN IT MEANS
PUSHING US TO GREATNESS
OR PULLING US FROM HARM.

FRIENDSHIP
LASTS WHEN IT
IS NOURISHED
WITH **LOVE.**

YOU AND I ALWAYS END UP

SINGING THE SAME TUNE.

FRIENDS HANG
ON OUR EVERY
WORD—NO
MATTER HOW
SHOCKING.

Friends help us see things from a different PERSPECTIVE.

FRIENDS
KNOW THAT
ARMS ARE
FOR HUGGING.

FRIENDS ALWAYS HAVE YOUR BACK.

EVERY
FRIENDSHIP
REQUIRES
SOME HEALTHY
DISTANCE.

Friends **LISTEN** to what you say and **HEAR** what you don't say.

THE BEST MIRROR IS AN OLD FRIEND.

GEORGE HERBERT

Sometimes friends are just two people **MAD** at the same person.

FRIENDS DON'T
HATE YOU
BECAUSE YOU'RE
BEAUTIFUL.

FRIENDS
LOVE YOU,

WARTS
AND ALL.

A TRUE FRIEND
PRAISES YOU IN
YOUR ABSENCE,
AND SAVES ANY
CRITICISM FOR
YOUR EARS ALONE.

PHOTO CREDITS